ONE ON A WEB
Counting Animals at Home

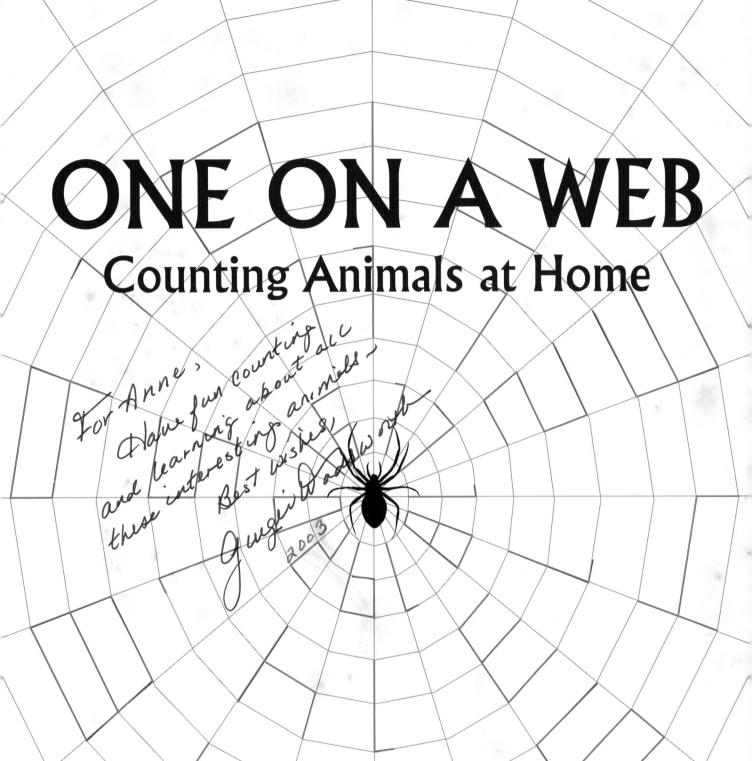

For Anne,
Have fun counting
and learning about all
these interesting animals.
Best wishes,
Ginger Wadsworth
2003

Ginger Wadsworth • Illustrated by James M. Needham

Charlesbridge

To Matt . . . one on a rock
—G. W.

For those parents and teachers who make learning fun
—J. N.

Text copyright © 1997 by Ginger Wadsworth
Illustrations copyright © 1997 by Charlesbridge Publishing

Published by Charlesbridge Publishing
85 Main Street, Watertown, MA 02172 (617) 926-0329

Printed in the United States of America
(hc) 10 9 8 7 6 5 4 3 2 1
(sc) 10 9 8 7 6 5 4 3 2 1

Library of Congress Cataloging-in-Publication Data
Wadsworth, Ginger.
One on a web/ by Ginger Wadsworth; illustrated by James M. Needham.
p.   cm.
Summary: Presents information about the habits and habitats of twenty common animals,
such as the robin, puppy, bee, and penguin, while counting from one to twenty.
ISBN 0-88106-971-X (reinforced for library use)
ISBN 0-88106-973-6 (softcover)
1. Counting—Juvenile literature. 2. Animals—Juvenile literature.
[1. Animals. 2. Counting.] I. Needham, James M., ill. II. Title.
QA113.W3   1997
591—dc20   96-35946 [E]

1

One hungry spider runs along
the edge of her web.

All spiders have eight legs. Most spiders release a strong
thread, called silk, from the back of their bodies. They use
the silk to wrap their eggs, to make webs, and to trap their
food. Some webs are only a single thread. Others are formed
in designs, like wheels or tunnels. Spiders eat the insects
and other bugs that get caught in their webs.

Two masked raccoons sleep next to each other in a hollow log.

2 Raccoons live in many places—the country, forests, and cities. They are awake during the night and that is when they look for food. Using their front paws, they eat fruits, vegetables, and insects. They even dip their long fingers into streams and lakes to find frogs and crayfish to eat. At sunrise raccoons look for a safe spot to sleep. They want a place that is quiet and dark, such as a cozy hollow log.

3

Three baby robins wait for worms in their nest.

Robins build bowl-shaped nests in trees and bushes. They make nests with their beaks, adding sticks, grass, and almost anything else they can find, even hair and scraps of paper. The mother robin lays several blue eggs. When the eggs first hatch, the babies are bald. They soon grow feathers, learn how to fly, and leave the nest.

Four sleek beavers swim toward their lodge.

4

Beavers cut down trees and branches near streams and lakes with their sharp teeth. They pull and push the wood into the water. With stones and mud, the beavers build a dome-shaped lodge out of trees and branches. The beaver family lives inside the lodge.

5

Five red fox pups
dash into their den.

Young foxes yip and bark as they play in front of their den. Their den is a hole in the ground at the edge of the forest. The foxes learn to capture and eat small mice and grasshoppers. They sleep in the den with their bushy tails covering their feet and noses like blankets. The den remains cool in hot weather, and it shelters the foxes during the winter.

6

Six red hens tuck their heads under their wings in their coop.

At night hens sleep side by side in their coop. Their "little house" has a roof to keep out the hot sun and the rain. The hens lay eggs in clean straw nests. In the fenced-in yard, they peck corn, wheat, and seeds, as well as juicy bugs.

Seven prairie dogs yip and yowl in their town.

7

Several thousand prairie dogs can live together in a town. Mounds of dirt dot the prairie. The prairie dogs move the dirt with their feet. Then they pack the earth down with their noses and foreheads. They dig tunnels underground that connect to little rooms. The prairie dogs sleep, eat, raise their young, and find shelter from rain, snow, and heat in these underground rooms. They dart into their town to escape from enemies such as coyotes, owls, and eagles.

Eight ponies chew hay in their stable.

8

Ponies are smaller than horses and just the right size for young riders. Like horses, ponies have one big toe on each foot and it is covered by a hoof. Ponies can walk, trot, canter, or even gallop on their short, strong legs. They usually have heavy coats and long manes and tails. Sometimes ponies stick their necks over the stable door and whinny for a carrot or an apple as a treat.

9 Nine newborn puppies doze together in their cardboard box.

The puppies lie next to their brothers and sisters in the box. They need lots of sleep and lots of their mother's milk because they are growing very fast. When they are a few days old, they open their eyes for the first time. Every day they get a little bigger. Before long they begin to play with one another and chew on the box!

10

Some bees build hives in nature. Other bees use man-made hives. No matter where they live, bees are always busy. During the day some of them fly from flower to flower gathering yellow pollen on their hind legs. They also collect flower nectar to make into honey and wax inside their hive. Other bees stay in the hive to clean and repair it. These worker bees feed the young—called larvae—until they grow into adult bees.

Eleven black-and-white cows walk to the barn to be milked.

11

Cows need grass to make milk. All day they eat, chewing their food slowly. They have four parts to their stomachs. The grass moves from part to part while it is being digested. Grass makes the cows grow strong and healthy, and it helps them make milk. The cows walk to the barn twice a day and stand patiently while they are milked.

12

Twelve piglets wallow in a puddle in their pen.

To cool off, pigs lie in water on hot days. When it is cold, they lie close together because they do not have enough hair to keep them warm. On other days they root, or dig, in the ground with their snouts. Piglets like to chase their mother around the pen and butt against her side until she lets them drink her milk.

Thirteen furry bats hang
upside down in their cave.

13

Bats sleep during the day, and at sunset they wake up.
They beat their wings and fly through the night sky.
Bats make clicking sounds that echo off everything in
their path. These sounds bounce back to the bats' ears
and help them find flying insects in the darkness. The
bats swoop up the insects with their wings and eat
them. When the sun rises, the bats return to their
cave. Side by side, they hang by their feet, asleep in
the cave until sunset.

Fourteen penguins slip and slide across their icy rookery.

Penguins gather in rookeries to mate, breed, and raise their young. They waddle on ice or rocky places near the sea. Layers of fat and thick waterproof feathers cover them so that they can live in subzero weather. They lay eggs on the ice or in scooped-out holes. After the penguin chicks are born, the rookery is more crowded than ever.

15

Fifteen woolly white sheep graze on grass in their pasture.

Sheep eat grass and chew it slowly as they graze in their fenced pasture. People raise sheep for their milk, meat, and wool. After the wool grows thick and long, it is sheared off, spun into yarn, and woven into cloth. It does not hurt the sheep to be sheared, and the wool grows back in a few months.

16 Sixteen sleepy rabbits snuggle side by side in their warren.

Many different kinds of rabbits live all over the world, except in Antarctica. They live on farms and in the wild. Wild rabbits dig underground tunnels, or warrens, with their front paws and powerful hind feet. Warrens protect rabbits from the heat and cold. During the cool part of the day, rabbits eat plants, grasses, and herbs. They run into their warren to escape enemies such as foxes, coyotes, bobcats, hawks, and human hunters. Rabbits also make great pets!

17

Seventeen shiny black ants carry a leaf to their colony.

Ants are insects that live and work together in underground colonies. Each ant has a job. Some ants gather food. Others take care of the baby ants. Ants dig tunnels and little rooms in the ground. The ants carry all the dirt to the surface. Beneath the ground, thousands of ants are busy at their jobs inside their colony.

Eighteen doves settle down for the night in their roost.

18

Doves are gray, ground-loving birds. During the day they peck the ground for seeds and small bugs. They bathe in small pools of water. They call "coo-ca-coo" to one another. At night they gather on long tree branches above the ground to sleep. The leaves on the branches shelter the doves from the wind and rain and hide them from their enemies, like bobcats

Nineteen oysters rest in their bed.

19

As seawater washes over the bed, the oysters swallow their food, tiny plants and animals. The oysters are permanently attached to the sea floor. When they sense danger, they close their twin shells tight around their soft bodies. This keeps a starfish from sucking out their tasty insides.

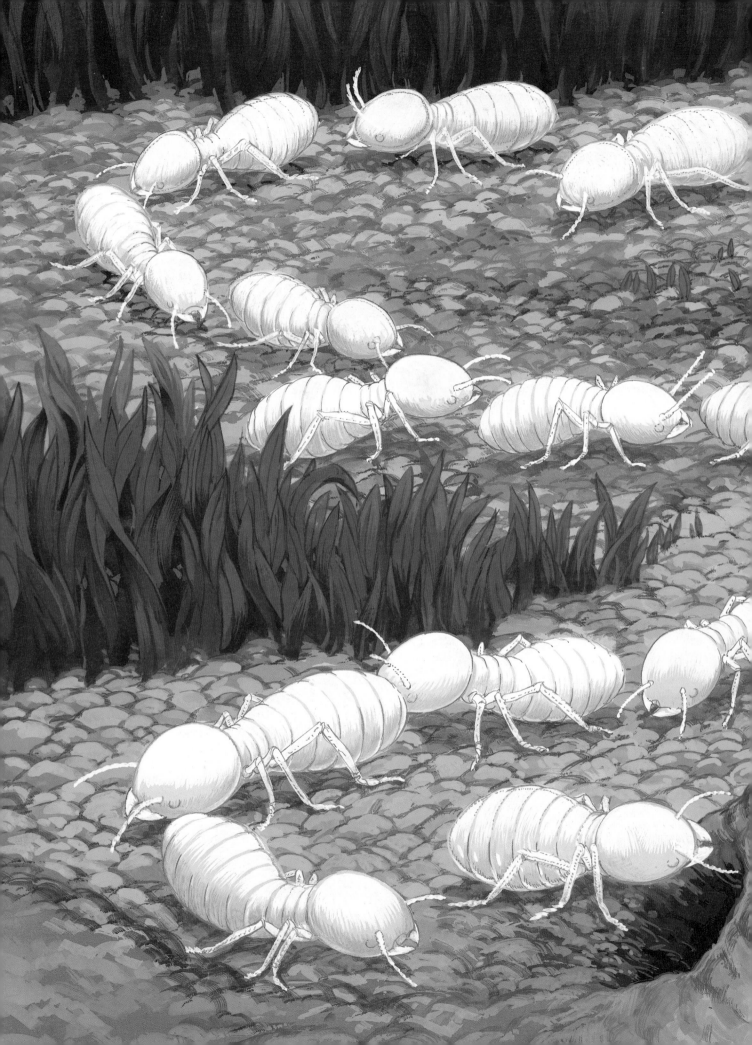

Twenty fast-moving termites scurry to their mound.

20

Termites are usually pale and have soft bodies. Like all insects, their bodies are divided into three parts: the head, thorax, and abdomen. Some termites build tall mounds. They are made of bits of wood, clay, and earth cemented together with termite saliva. The thick walls of the mounds protect the termites from the hot sun and from enemies like the anteater, with its long, quick tongue.

The
illustrations
in this book are
done in gouache
on Crescent
illustration board.
The display type and
text type were set in
Souvenir and Flare.
Color separations were
made by Pure Imaging,
Watertown, Massachusetts.
Printed and bound by
Worzalla Publishing Company,
Stevens Point, Wisconsin
This book was printed
on recycled paper.
Production supervision by
Brian G. Walker
Designed by
Diane M. Earley